D1809834

# SMOKING AND LIBERTY

Pour Sarah
my girl in England
que j'embrasse

partout

Pierre
27 mars 2002

# Also by Pierre Lemieux

*Du libéralisme à l'anarcho-capitalisme* (Paris: Presses Universitaires de France, 1983); Japanese translation, Tokyo: Shunju Sha, 1990.

*La souveraineté de l'individu* (Paris: Presses Universitaires de France, 1987); Spanish translation, Madrid: Union Editorial, 1992.

*L'anarcho-capitalisme* (Paris: Presses Universitaires de France, 1988); Turkish translation, Istanbul: Iletisim Yayincilik AS, 1994.

*Apologie des sorcières modernes* (Paris: Belles Lettres, 1991).

*Le droit de porter des armes* (Paris: Belles Lettres, 1993).

Pierre Lemieux

# Smoking and Liberty

Government as a
Public Health Problem

*Published in cooperation with the*
*Texas Public Policy Foundation*

Varia Press
P. O. Box 35040, RPO Fleury
Montreal, Quebec
Canada H2C 3K4

Telephone: (514) 389-8448
Fax: (514) 389-0128

**Canadian Cataloguing in Publication Data:**

Lemieux, Pierre, 1947-

Smoking and Liberty

Translation of: Tabac et liberté.
Includes bibliographical references.

ISBN 2-922245-01-2

1. Cigarette smokers.   2. Tobacco - Physiological effect.
3. Passive smoking.   4. Smoking - Government policy.
5. Liberty.   I. Title.

HV5751.L4513 1996       363.4       C96-941514-1

*Design, typesetting and mounting:*
Guy Verville, Info-Typographer

*Photo:*
Pierre Lemieux by Serge Caron,
Le Photo-Maître (Outremont, Quebec)

© Varia Press, 1997
All rights reserved for all countries.

ISBN 2-922245-01-2
*Third Printing*

Legal deposit: 1ˢᵗ quarter 1997
National Library of Canada
Bibliothèque nationale du Québec

*Printed in Canada*

# Contents

☒ ✳ ☒

*The habit of smoking is disgusting to sight, repulsive to smell, dangerous to the brain, noxious to the lung, spreading its fumes around the smoker as foul as those that come from Hell.*

James I (1604), quoted by Richard Klein,
*Cigarettes are Sublime* (Durham and London:
Duke University Press, 1993)

*Aristotle and the philosophers can say what they like, but there is nothing equal to tobacco: it's an honest man's habit, and anyone who can get on without it doesn't deserve to be living at all.*

Sganarelle in Molière, *Dom Juan*, Act I, Scene 1

*If it feels good, it must be bad.*

*Fortune*, October 21, 1991

# Prologue

The smoking debate is quite indicative of a certain way of viewing political power. In just a few years, a theory has spread like wild fire: smoking is dangerous for smokers and nonsmokers alike; therefore, state intervention is warranted whatever the cost in terms of individual liberty.

What I plan to do here is to probe the assumptions underlying this approach. More precisely, I will raise three questions. First, has tobacco been proven medically dangerous beyond any reasonable doubt? Second, assuming that the answer is yes, does this justify state intervention? Third, does the regulation of tobacco by the state carry with it hidden costs from the standpoint of individual liberty?

In contrast with governmental studies on these questions, I will first state the biases that could affect my analysis. I first admit a personal bias: as I am presently a smoker myself, I would prefer to think that the pleasure of tobacco is not dangerous to my health. My second bias is philosophical: I greatly value individual liberty, and I believe that when it clashes with authoritarian restrictions, the burden of proof lies with authority. However, despite these biases, I will try to provide an objective analysis of the issues.

# 1.

## A Few Doubts about the Danger of Tobacco

**D**oes smoking cause disease and death? This is not an easy question, as I am neither a biologist, nor a pathologist, nor an epidemiologist. And noting how health scientists treat economic and political questions, I am leery of committing against their sciences the same offenses which they commit against economics and political science. Therefore, I will limit my inquiry to a much narrower question: To what extent is science unanimous about the health risks of tobacco?

## *Is Smoking Dangerous for the Smoker?*

A non-specialist who surveys the scientific literature is rapidly persuaded that the vast majority of authors agree that tobacco is dangerous for the smoker's health. Since the 1950s, and especially since the 1980s, a large number of scientific studies suggest a causal relation between smoking and a certain number of pulmonary and cardiovascular diseases.[1] One can find critics, though, who do not march to the same drummer. In his book, *Smoking and Common Sense*, a Danish physician, Dr. Tage Voss, states that "It has never been dem-

---

1 Surveys of relevant research and results can be found in Surgeon General, *Preventing Tobacco Use Among Young People: Report of the Surgeon General* (U.S. Government Printing Office, 1994), pp. 15-30. See also Ernst L. Wynder and Dietrich Hoffmann, Smoking and Lung Cancer: Scientific Challenges and Opportunities, *Cancer Research*, Vol. 54, No. 20 (October 15, 1994), pp. 5284-5295; and Michael C. Fiore (Ed.), *Cigarette Smoking: A Clinical Guide to Assessment and Treatment, The Medical Clinics of North America*, Vol. 76, No. 2 (March 1992).

onstrated that tobacco smoking leads to cancer."[2] Are we really all that sure that tobacco causes health problems? The two keywords here are "cause" and "sure:"

First, consider lung cancer. If a real causal relation were established, then all smokers would eventually get lung cancer. Now, although the majority of those who get lung cancer (estimates range from 80% to 90%[3]) were smokers, it does not follow that most smokers develop this disease: actually, only 10% of smokers develop lung cancer. Moreover, a small proportion of nonsmokers are also victims of lung

---

2 Tage Voss, *Smoking and Common Sense: One Doctor's View* (London: Peter Owen, 1992), p. 46. The author continues: "Researchers have never succeeded in producing lung cancer in animal experiments, not even in guinea pigs living the majority of their lives in a highly concentrated tobacco atmosphere." See also James T. Bennet and Thomas J. Dilorenzo, *Official Lies: How Washington Misleads Us* (Alexandria: Groom Books, 1992), p. 227.

3 U.S. Environmental Protection Agency, *Respiratory Health Effects of Passive Smoking: Lung Cancer and Other Disorders* (Washington, D.C.: December 1992), pp. 1-6 and 2-1; Ministère de la Santé et des Services sociaux, *Une législation québécoise contre le tabagisme. Un choix pour la santé* (Government of Quebec, 1995), p. 12.

cancer.[4] If all diseases that are said to be tobacco-related are added up, about half of today's smokers will not die from any of them.[5] By themselves, these facts do not contradict the hypothesis of a causal relation, for we may still suppose that all smokers would have died of a "tobacco-related" disease if they had not already died from some other cause. But using this logic, we might as well suppose that nonsmokers would also have died from a tobacco-related disease, if only the Parcae had not brought them down in some other way.

Other facts raise doubts as to the causal link between smoking and so-called tobacco-related diseases. There are countries with high tobacco consumption and low incidence of lung cancer, and vice versa. Although Japanese men have long smoked

---

4 H.J. Eysenck, *Smoking, Personality, and Stress: Psychosocial Factors in the Prevention of Cancer and Coronary Heart Disease*, New York, Springer-Verlag, 1991, p. 1. See also U.S. Environmental Protection Agency, *op. cit.*, p. 1-6 and 2-1; Ministère de la Santé et des Services sociaux, *op. cit.*, p. 12.

5 Health Canada, *Tobacco Control: A Blueprint to Protect the Health of Canadians* (Ottawa: Government of Canada, 1995), p. 1.

more than American men, it has been observed that the incidence of lung cancer is twice as high among the latter as among the former.[6] Between 1950 and 1980, the incidence of lung cancer was many times higher in Austria than in Japan, even though tobacco consumption was lower in the former country.[7] Finns are twice as likely to develop lung cancer as Americans, although the latter smoke twice as much.[8]

Although the Greeks have one of the highest per capita smoking rates in the world, their country shows a relatively low incidence of lung cancer. The U.S. *Environmental Protection Agency* explains this paradox by citing high fruit consumption in Greece[9]. The preventive effect of fruits —and vegetables—has been confirmed by

6 Ernst L. Wynder and Dietrich Hoffmann, Smoking and Lung Cancer: Scientific Challenges and Opportunities, *op. cit.*, pp. 5288-5289.

7 Tage Voss, *op. cit.*, p. 49.

8 Christopher Caldwell, Smoke Gets in Your Eyes, *The American Spectator* (May1992), p. 27.

9 U.S. Environmental Protection Agency, *op. cit.*, Annex 3.18.2, p. A-87.

epidemiological cancer research.[10] Antony Flew, a British philosopher, rightly wonders why American bureaucrats do not therefore recommend that smokers eat fruit instead of foregoing tobacco.[11]

One must also understand the limits of science. There is no satisfactory explanatory theory of cancer. The EPA recognizes that "the exact mechanisms and tobacco smoke components associated with these health effects are not known with certainty."[12] Our knowledge of the causes of tobacco-related diseases is based solely on statistical correlations. Not only are we not certain that a smoker will be a victim

---

10 Ernst L. Wynder and Dietrich Hoffmann, Smoking and Lung Cancer: Scientific Challenges and Opportunities, *op. cit.*, p. 5289-5290.

11 Antony Flew, *Passive Smoking, Scientific Method and Corrupted Science*, London, Freedom Organization For The Right to Enjoy Smoking Tobacco (FOREST), 1994, p. 3.

12 U.S. Environmental Protection Agency, *op. cit.*, p. 2-1. The complete quote is: "Although the exact mechanisms and tobacco smoke components associated with these health effects are not known with certainty, more than 40 known or suspected human carcinogens have been identified in tobacco smoke."

of tobacco-related diseases, but it is not statistically impossible that such diseases are caused by complementary or even completely different factors.[13]

Smoking is neither a necessary nor a sufficient condition for so-called tobacco-related diseases. It is not a necessary condition since many victims of such diseases are nonsmokers. It is not a sufficient condition because a large number of smokers do not develop them.[14] Among the epidemiologists' "confounding factors" that could explain all, or part of, smoking diseases, it has been observed that tobacco is more prevalent among low-income groups, and that smokers generally take more risks in life. For instance, they have riskier, more diversified sex lives. When one reflects on the more common prevalence of smoking among left-handers than

---

13 Ernst L. Wynder and Dietrich Hoffmann, *op. cit.*, p. 5287.
14 Hans J. Eysenck, *op. cit.*; and Hans J. Eysenck, Smoking and Health, in Robert D. Tollison (Ed.), *Smoking and Society: Toward a More Balanced Assessment*, (Lexington: Lexington Books, 1986), p. 17-88.

among right-handers, one suspects that what is viewed as the consequences of smoking tobacco might instead be related to smokers' heredity and psychological traits.[15]

The fact that life insurance companies discriminate against smokers confirms the reality of a negative correlation between tobacco and life expectancy, but it does not change statistics into causality. Similarly, when automobile insurance companies discovered a correlation between a poor credit record and the amount of insurance claims,[16] this did not show that the first factor causes the second. Statistical correlations may be enough for an insurance company to calculate the correct premium to charge for a policy, but they will not satisfy a critical mind inquiring into the

---

15 Christopher Caldwell, Smoke Gets in Your Eyes, *op. cit.*, p. 26-27; Surgeon General, *op. cit.*, Table 28, p. 91. On the general topic of smoking and personality, see H.J. Eysenck, *Smoking, Personality, and Stress: Psychosocial Factors in the Prevention of Cancer and Coronary Heart Disease* (New York: Springer-Verlag, 1991).

16 *Wall Street Journal*, November 6, 1995, p. A1.

legitimacy of state-imposed limitations on individual freedoms.

As much as epidemiology points to tobacco among the causes of certain diseases, the very same science recognizes its prophylactic virtues. A recent review of epidemiological research concludes that "the evidence to date, taken as a whole, provides quite strong support for the notion that smoking, presumably through the action of nicotine, reduces the risk of AD [Alzheimer's disease]."[17] Another survey of the scientific literature by Morens *et al.* shows massive evidence (34 out of 35 studies published to date) that nicotine greatly reduces the risk of Parkinson's disease.[18]

Smokers also appear to be less likely to contract such diseases as intestinal cancer or

---

17 P.N. Lee, Smoking and Alzheimer's Disease: A Review of the Epidemiological Evidence, *Neuroepidemiology*, Vol. 13, No. 4 (July-August 1994), p. 143.

18 D.M. Morens, A. Grandinetti, D. Reed, L.R. White, and G.W. Ros, Cigarette smoking and protection from Parkinson's disease: False association or etiologic clue?, *Neurology*, Vol. 45, No. 6 (June 1995), p. 1041-1051.

diabetes, or to suffer from obesity.[19] A quarter, perhaps a third, of Americans are overweight, and thus at greater risk of high blood pressure, cardiovascular diseases, uterine and breast cancer, gall bladder disease, and diabetes. According to a *New England Journal of Medicine* study, some 300,000 American deaths each year are related to obesity, which is nearly as many as tobacco-related deaths.[20] Observing the number of fat people at U.S. airports, one would think that they should be compelled, instead of forbidden, to smoke. So long as we'll all die anyway, we're better off dying slim.

## How Dangerous Is Environmental Tobacco Smoke?

Given that the medical consequences of smoking are far from clear, one would

---

19 Tage Voss, *op. cit.*, pp. 54 and 59-60.
20 Larry Laudan, *The Book of Risks: Fascinating Facts About the Chances We Take Every Day* (New York: John Wily & Sons, 1994), p. 129; and Jacob Sullum, What the Doctor Orders, *Reason Magazine*, January 1996.

expect the effects of environmental tobacco smoke (or ETS) to be especially doubtful. Simply, nonsmokers exposed to ETS receive only minute doses of tobacco smoke—probably between 1/1000 or, at most, 1/100 of the smoker's dose.[21] According to a study published in the *International Archives of Occupational Environment Health*, one would have to spend between 11 and 50 hours in a heavily tobacco smoke-polluted environment in order to absorb as much nicotine as a smoker takes in from one cigarette. Moreover, ETS produces only a fraction of air pollutants, between 28% and 50% in restaurant smoking sections, for example.[22]

---

21 Donald J. Ecobichon and Joseph M. Wu (Eds.), *Environmental Tobacco Smoke: Proceedings of the International Symposium at McGill University 1989* (Toronto: Lexington, 1990), p. 229. ETS, or second-hand smoke, is tobacco smoke (mainly from the smoldering cigarette) that is not inhaled by the smoker and disperses in the air. Could it be that "second-hand smoke" was rechristened "environmental tobacco smoke" because of the politically-correct potential of putting the environment in the picture?

22 Christopher Caldwell, Smoke Gets in Your Eyes, *op. cit.*, p. 26.

Despite all this, the 1992 EPA report brought to the fore the idea that ETS threatens nonsmokers' health to such an extent that it merits classification amongst the most dangerous carcinogens, i.e., Group A or "Known Human Carcinogens." The EPA itself suggests that ETS gives nonsmokers 0.1% to 0.7% of the average smoker's dose of nicotine—less than one fifth of a cigarette daily; but the agency surmises that nonsmokers could receive up to 10% or 20% of the smoker's dose of other tobacco smoke components.[23] A University of California environmental health expert goes along with the maximum estimate by claiming that nonsmokers in an office smoking environment are subjected to a certain ETS carcinogen as if they smoked nearly four cigarettes daily.[24] At best, then, nonsmokers don't smoke; at

---

23 U.S. Environmental Protection Agency, *Respiratory Health Effects of Passive Smoking: Lung Cancer and Other Disorders* (Washington, D.C., December 1992), p. 3-53.

24 "The Truth About Secondhand Smoke", *Consumer Reports*, January 1995, p. 29.

worst, they smoke very lightly. How can the EPA conclude, therefore, that ETS causes disease and death?

Indeed, many critics have challenged the agency's conclusions. For one thing, it has been noted that the EPA rated ETS risks much more severely than other risks. The agency estimated that ETS carries a risk ratio of 1.19 for lung cancer, which means that exposure to ETS increases the lung cancer risk of a nonsmoker by 19%. Now, epidemiologists usually discard risk ratios smaller than 3.0. When the EPA calculated a risk ratio of 2.6 for diesel emissions, it only classified them as a Group B carcinogen, i.e., among "Probable Human Carcinogens." And when the agency calculated risk ratios above 3.0 for electromagnetic fields, it did not even feel justified to classify them as a probable carcinogen.[25]

If there is any risk with ETS, it is tiny compared to the ordinary risks of life. A study

---

25 Antony Flew, *op. cit.*, p. 3-4; and U.S. Environmental Protection Agency, *op. cit.*, *passim*.

conducted in Shanghai, in cooperation with researchers from the U.S. *National Cancer Institute*, concluded that lung cancer among women who cook with rapeseed oil is 2.5 times higher than among those who use soybean oil.[26] Another epidemiological study estimated that lung cancer risks are 6.7 times higher in houses where pet birds are kept—a risk ratio five times higher than ETS.[27] According to a U.S. government scientist, chlorinated water carries a higher cancer risk than ETS.[28] And if we believe the government estimate on the number of non-smoking Canadians who die from lung cancer caused by ETS, it is still only 1/9 of the number who die in transportation accidents, and approximately the same as those who drown.[29]

---

26 Christopher Caldwell, Smoke Gets in Your Eyes, *op. cit.*, p. 26.

27 Antony Flew, *op. cit.*, p. 4.

28 See Peter Samuel and Peter Spencer, Facts Catch Up with "Political" Science, *Consumers Research*, Vol. 76, No. 5 (May 1993).

29 Statistics on accidents compiled by Taylor Buckner (Concordia University), from 1991 *Juristat* data.

Even if the EPA has only produced rather small estimates for ETS risks, serious doubts have been raised regarding the scientific methodology they used.[30] The EPA considered 30 epidemiological studies on lung cancer among women married to smokers compared to those who were married to nonsmokers. Only six of these studies found a low but statistically significant correlation between lung cancer and marriage to a smoker. The EPA discarded all but 11 of the studies, which were then aggregated using a controversial method called "meta-analysis."[31] Some critics claim that, in order to finally yield the

---

30 John C. Luik, Pandoras Box: The Dangers of Politically Corrupted Science for Democratic Public Policy, *Bostonia*; reprinted by FOREST under the title: *Through the Smokescreen of "Science": The Dangers of Politically Corrupted Science for Democratic Public Policy* (London: 1994); Michael Fumento, Is EPA Blowing Its Own Smoke? How Much Science Is Behind Its Tobacco Finding?, *Investors Business Daily*, January 28, 1993, p. 1 ff.; Peter Samuel and Peter Spencer, Facts Catch Up With "Political Science", *op. cit.* See also U.S. Environmental Protection Agency, *op. cit.*, p. 1-11.

31 Alvin R. Feinstein, Justice, Science and the "Bad Guys", *Toxicologic Pathology*, Vol. 20, No. 2 (1992), pp. 289-303.

incriminating results, the EPA also used unusual statistical significance rates and a biased statistical test.

Although the EPA's claims have been adopted by nearly all public authorities in the world, they remain very controversial within the scientific community. Robert Barro, the well-known economist, writes: "Despite the recent assertions by the EPA, the statistical evidence for health risks from secondhand smoke is extremely weak, even by the standards of an empirical economist."[32] Others have used stronger words to describe the EPA work—like "politically corrupted science," "rotten science", and "bogus science."[33]

The non-specialist can easily find serious epidemiological studies, published by recognized scientists in established journals, that find no relation between

---

32 Robert Barro, Send Regulations Up in Smoke, *Wall Street Journal*, June 3, 1994, p. A-14.
33 John C. Luik, *op. cit.*, p. 3, 8, and *passim*.

ETS and cancer.[34] In 1989, at a time when the EPA was declaring war on ETS, McGill University hosted an international scientific conference where more than 80 specialists presented and discussed papers on this question. One of the organizers, Dr. Joseph M. Wu, writes in the conclusion of the proceedings: "One of the most striking consensus views emanating from this conference is that the published data, when critically examined and evaluated, are inconsistent with the notion that ETS is a health hazard."[35] The papers presented at another scientific conference on ETS, held in Tokyo in 1993, conclude in a similar vein, one after another: "It is clear that the epidemiological evidence does not convincingly support the notion that ETS

---

34 See Ernst L. Wynder and Dietrich Hoffmann, Smoking and Lung Cancer: Scientific Challenges and Opportunities, *op. cit.*, p. 5291.

35 Joseph M. Wu, Summary and Concluding Remarks, in Donald J. Ecobichon and Joseph M. Wu (Ed.), *Environmental Tobacco Smoke: Proceedings of the International Symposium at McGill University 1989* (Toronto: Lexington Books, 1990), p. 375.

exposure causes lung cancer."[36] Concerning
the effects of ETS on children's pulmonary health, another participant concludes: "In my opinion, the scientific data
do not support the conclusions of the
EPA."[37] Two of the authors are rather
more affirmative: "The U.S. EPA report is
a good illustration of the propagation of
weak arguments and speculative calcula-
tions in place of real information."[38]

Of course, one can also find epidemiological studies leading to the opposite conclusions. Therefore, we must ask
which side has more weight in the balance
of evidence? Strangely enough, on this
point defenders and enemies of tobacco
seem to agree. On one side, the tobacco

---

36 P.N. Lee, An Assessment of the Epidemiological Evidence
Relating Lung Cancer Risk in Never Smokers to Environ-
mental Tobacco Smoke, in H. Kasuga (Ed.), *Environmental
Tobacco Smoke* (New York: Springer-Verlag, 1993), p. 65.

37 Alan J. Gross, Respiratory Disease and ETS, in H. Kasuga,
*op. cit.*, p. 86.

38 Paul Switzer and Maxwell W. Layard, Problems in the
Assessment of Lung Cancer Risk from Exposure to Environmental Tobacco Smoke, in H. Kasuga, *op. cit.*, p. 108.

industry claims that 80% of epidemiological studies on ETS and lung cancer show no positive and statistically significant correlation.[39] On the other side, antitobacco activists admit that only seven of the actual 33 epidemiological studies, i.e., 21%, find a positive and statistically significant correlation between smoking and lung cancer.[40]

As far as other tobacco-related diseases are concerned, the evidence is at least as controversial.[41] The causal link is especially doubtful in the case of more benign diseases or for allergies. There are some who claim that tobacco's allergenic properties have never been demonstrated, or even that ETS actually decreases bronchial constriction.[42]

---

39 British-American Tobacco Company Limited, *Environmental Tobacco Smoke*, undated, p. 10.
40 The Truth About Secondhand Smoke, *Consumer Reports*, January 1995, p. 28.
41 Donald J. Ecobichon and Joseph M. Wu (Ed.), *op. cit.*, especially p. xvii, 149, 181, 220, 262, and 301.
42 Christopher Caldwell, Smoke Gets in Your Eyes, *op. cit.*, p. 25.

## *Official Lies*

One may therefore be rightly suspicious of the official orthodoxy concerning tobacco, and especially ETS. Are public authorities lying? Could it be that federal advertisements about ETS wreaking havoc are just so much hot air?

It would not be the first time that political authorities lied to their subjects, either by ignoring or by manipulating science. History knows of a number of famous cases: the prosecution of Galileo, witch-hunts in the 16th and 17th centuries, Lyssenko's biology… And one must not forget all those little daily lies and broken promises that naturally flow from reasons of state and myopic politicians.

The "Lalonde doctrine" illustrates how science is scorned for reasons of state. In a 1974 booklet published by the Canadian Department of National Health and Welfare, and signed by then minister Marc Lalonde, a chapter entitled "Science Versus

Health Promotion" starts with these words: "The spirit of inquiry and skepticism, and particularly the Scientific Method, so essential to research, are, however, a problem in health promotion. The reason for this fact is that science is full of 'ifs', 'buts' and 'maybes' while messages designed to influence the public must be loud, clear and unequivocal."[43] "But," the author adds, "many of Canada's health problems are sufficiently pressing that action has to be taken on them even if all the scientific evidence is not in." We are told that, in fact, scientific prudence and skepticism may even be harmful: "The scientific 'yes, but' is essential to research but for modifying the behavior of the population it sometimes produces the 'uncertain sound' that is all the excuse needed by many to cultivate and tolerate an environment and lifestyle that is hazardous to health."[44] In

---

43 Marc Lalonde, *A New Perspective on the Health of Canadians: A Working Document* (Ottawa: Department of National Health and Welfare, 1974), p. 57.

44 *Ibid.*, p. 58.

other words, when the state is intent on "modifying the behavior of the population," it does not really matter whether the supporting hypotheses are valid or not.

Instead of simply ignoring science *à la* Lalonde, Power is often tempted to manipulate it. When God was in fashion, Power relied on religious justifications; now that science is God, Power corrupts science. Future historians will probably recall the EPA's theories on asbestos, radon or ETS as classic instances of the political manipulation of science. An EPA-appointed panel of experts notes that the agency is not very strong on science anyway: "Indeed, scientists play a minor role inside the agency, which tends to be dominated by lawyers and other non-scientists."[45]

Although the infamy cast on tobacco may be partly explained by our natural fear

---

45 Quoted by Peter Samuel and Peter Spencer, Facts Catch Up With "Political Science", *op. cit.*, p. 10.

of disease and death as well as our tendency to look for scapegoats and panaceas, the irrationality of it all remains striking. Bertrand Deveaud and Bertrand Lemennicier have observed that by adding together the proportions of lung cancers traced to tobacco (85%), radon (30%), and working conditions (40%), 155% of the cases of lung cancer are accounted for.[46]

The Quebec government dived into these fads with its characteristic lack of critical spirit. Its 1995 working paper charges tobacco with responsibility in nearly all diseases it can come up with, including breast cancer. At least, it does not always pretend to be scientific, as when the authors write: "Protecting our community against tobacco promoters' commercial and financial interests and against ETS, calls for state intervention and turns

---

46 Bertrand Deveaud and Bertrand Lemennicier, *Tabac. L'histoire d'une imposture* (Paris: Jacques Grancher, 1994), p. 71.

smoking into a political question."[47] To put it mildly, this report is nothing but propaganda.

The historical interest of the Prince to fool his subjects does not fundamentally change in the hands of the political and bureaucratic processes that rule a democratic system such as ours, as these processes do not necessarily lead to Power's frankness and unselfish search for truth. Given the complexity of political choices, the difficulty of unraveling their consequences, and the voters' rational ignorance, there is not much sanction against a politician's self-interest in blatantly disregarding the truth. Another factor pushing in the same direction is the influence of special interest groups, which are not only found on the tobacco industry's side of the debate.

---

47 Ministère de la Santé et des Services sociaux, *op. cit.*, especially pp. 12 and 21: "La protection de la collectivité contre les intérêts commerciaux et financiers des promoteurs du tabac et contre la fumée dans l'air ambiant interpelle l'État et fait du tabagisme une question politique."

The health bureaucracy—which includes civil servants but also employees and researchers of subsidized organizations—is one of the most powerful interest groups, and one that has the most to win in this battle. These bureaucrats' influence, careers and remuneration often depend on their success in persuading the public that there exist serious problems crying out for state intervention, such as smoking.[48] It would be naive to think that anti-tobacco activists are less self-interested than their opponents. Stanton Glantz, an activist retained by the EPA to work on its 1992 report, organizes smoking cessation seminars for a living. He writes: "The main thing the science has done on the issue of ETS, in addition to help people like me pay mortgages, is it has legitimized the concerns that people have that they don't

---

48 Robert D. Tollison (Ed.), *Cleaning the Air: Perspectives on Environmental Tobacco Smoke* (Lexington: Lexington Books, 1988), p. 92 sq.

like cigarette smoke."[49] Indeed, the assumption that public bureaucrats, like everybody else, are motivated by their own self-interest forms the basis of the new theories of bureaucracy.[50]

Of course, self-interest is not the only explanatory factor. There are certainly well-meaning individuals who are deeply convinced that they are furthering the common good when they contribute to the politicization of science and to the state regulation of tobacco. In this, they have benefited from the support of public opinion, which has come to accept that the state may impose its own conception of the good. This phenomenon is related to what Philippe Bénéton has called "the scourge of good."[51]

The performance of state power in the search for, and propagation of, truth is so

---

49 Stanton Glantz, quoted by Christopher Caldwell, Smoke Gets in Your Eyes, *op. cit.*, p. 28.

50 William A. Niskanen, *Bureaucracy and Representative Government* (Chicago: Adline-Atherton, 1971).

51 Philippe Bénéton, *Le fléau du bien. Essai sur les politiques sociales occidentales 1960-1980* (Paris: Laffont, 1983).

bleak that, other things being equal, the wise man is less likely to err by rejecting the official truths publicized by state propaganda than by swallowing them.

# 2.

## If Tobacco Is Dangerous, Should It Be Controlled?

**B**ut let's forget everything I have said thus far, and suppose instead that public health arguments against tobacco are scientifically grounded. The question, then, is whether they justify government prohibition or regulation of tobacco. It is important to realize that there is only a difference of degree between prohibition and regulation: prohibition is extreme regulation, and mere regulation requires prohibition in specified circumstances. I will look at state intervention in tobacco, first, from the viewpoint of the smokers' own good, and then from the perspective of protecting nonsmokers.

## *Protecting Smokers*

Smoking carries costs for smokers. Economically, a cost is what is foregone when one chooses one alternative (smoking, for instance) over another (not smoking). Smoking costs include the purchase of tobacco products, and also the health costs which might be incurred as a result of the practice. Health costs are defined as the increased probability of developing one tobacco related disease or another, multiplied by the loss of satisfaction that would follow. Although lost satisfaction is often estimated in monetary terms—i.e., as lost income—it also includes less measurable components like physical pain or discomfort, psychological distress, fear of death, etc.

Many consumption activities carry risks of disease or accidents. In France, a few dozen of people die each year in skiing or mountaineering accidents. In 1991, accidental falls accounted for the deaths of 2,053 Canadians, while five were killed by lightning.[52] Other examples are easy to come by. Individuals voluntarily accept these costs—in skiing, house repairs, driving, etc.—because they consider the benefits of such activities to be higher than their costs. Life is full of choices that require a continuous balancing of costs and benefits, of what is lost and what is gained in terms of satisfaction.

The question is, Who will evaluate the costs and benefits of what an individual decides to do, or not to do? Once it is realized that these costs and benefits are subjective, that an individual's preferences reside in his own mind, the obvious answer

---

52  Taylor Buckner (Concordia University), from 1991 *Juristat* data.

is that each individual—each adult, at any rate—is better able than anybody else to determine his own cost-benefit ratio. Even if such individual evaluations are not perfect, the individual himself is presumably better placed than anybody else to know his own preferences.

The benefits of smoking are essentially subjective, just like the benefits of skiing, drinking wine, driving, or anything we consume or do. The very fact that an individual smokes tobacco means that, given his own circumstances, he thinks that his benefits exceed his costs—that he gets a net benefit from the experience. This is not to say, of course, that the smoker's subjective benefits have no objective and measurable features. We have already noted the probable prophylactic benefits of smoking, especially in relation to Alzheimer's and Parkinson's diseases. We might add that the favorable effects of smoking on cortical arousal level, concentration and relaxation are apparently well-founded scientific facts.[53]

Although it is pretty obvious that one will not freely do something that entails only costs and no benefit, anti-tobacco activists—like prohibitionists in general —tend to ignore the benefit side in the cost-benefit balance. An interesting illustration of this error can be found in a book entitled *The Economic Costs of Smoking and Benefits of Quitting*, in which the authors try to estimate the costs of tobacco-related diseases, but nowhere mention the benefits of smoking. They calculate the benefits of smoking cessation as simply the costs avoided, and conclude that "it literally pays to quit smoking."[54] This is like saying that

---

53 H.J. Eysenck, *op. cit.*, p. 88: "Among the positive features of smoking, which have now been firmly established by research (O'Connor & Stravynski, 1982), are its ability to raise the cortical arousal level and thus counteract boredom and fatigue; its ability to make anxious persons relax […]; and its power to increase attention and vigilance…"

54 Gary Osler, Graham A. Colditz and Nancy L. Kelly, *The Economic Costs of Smoking and Benefits of Quitting* (Lexington: Lexington Books, 1984), p. 124.

it pays to turn off the furnace during the winter because it saves heating costs and reduces the risk of fire.

On what basis is the state justified in limiting the individual's freedom to make his own trade-off between the costs and benefits of smoking? Paternalism is the obvious answer. As the argument goes, individuals are either not equipped or not competent enough to decide what's good for themselves, and therefore the state must intervene to make such decisions for them.[55] The crudest version of paternalism assumes that the state is to citizens what parents are to their children, or what tutors are to their wards. For, indeed, in order to make people behave in the way it chooses, state paternalism resorts not to persuasion but to force (even if only the tax collector's force). The cruder versions of

---

55 See Douglas J. Den Uyl, Smoking, Human Rights, and Civil Liberties, in Robert D. Tollison (Ed.), *Smoking and Society: Toward a More Balanced Assessment* (Lexington: Lexington Books, 1986), p. 189-213.

state paternalism are somewhat difficult to defend in a free society.

Paternalism therefore comes in more sophisticated versions, one of which is the "imperfect information" argument. Consumers—smokers in our case—it is said, cannot reach enlightened decisions because they lack proper information. The state intervenes only to inform them, or to correct their mistaken choices.

Three objections can be immediately made to this kind of rationalization. First, it is doubtful that people underestimate the health risks of smoking; actually, they overestimate them, when compared to scientific opinions on the subject. While the actual probability of a smoker dying of lung cancer is no higher than 10%, a scientific opinion poll analyzed by Professor Kip Viscusi in the *Journal of Political Economy* shows that public perception places this at 42.6% on average, and that only 9.7% of the public believes the risk is lower than 10%. The public's overestimation of the risk of dying of one of the other tobacco-related illnesses may be less striking, but the average perception is still two to three times higher than the scientifically estimated risk of 18% to 36%.[56] Second, there is nothing to suggest that information supplied by the state will be more exact or truer than whatever is available to consumers in the market. Finally, information is a good, much like any other. Perfect information is as rare as, say, the perfect automobile. A consumer will get information up to the point where he estimates that its marginal value is not worth its marginal cost. On what basis, other than paternalism, could the state determine that people do not purchase or obtain enough information in the market? Or should we say that, since all activities of life require

---

56 W. Kip Viscusi, Do Smokers Underestimate Risks? *Journal of Political Economy*, Vol. 98, No. 6 (1990), p. 1253-1269; and, by the same author, *Smoking: Making the Risky Decision* (New York: Oxford University Press, 1992), p. 61 ff.

information, the state should therefore control not only tobacco consumption but also what people read, whom they marry, how they raise their children, and so forth?

Another justification for state paternalism is based on the idea that tobacco is an addictive drug. Now, addiction is difficult to define and measure, and its physiological conditions as well as its variations among individuals are controversial matters.[57] What is certain is that smoking habits are not impossible to break, as more than half of the 66% of non-smoking Quebecers are former smokers.[58] In fact, every good thing (in the eye of the beholder) generates a form of addiction, even if it has no direct pharmacological effects: fine cuisine, sports, writing, love and (perhaps) marriage are but a few examples.

Economists would define addiction as a situation where the marginal utility (or

---

57 See, among others, Tage Voss, *op. cit.*, p. 87-92; and *Wall Street Journal*, March 23, 1995, p. B1.

58 Ministère de la Santé et des Services sociaux, *op. cit.*, p. 7.

satisfaction) of a given good is increased by its past consumption. The hypothesis that tobacco is addictive in this sense has been empirically, and successfully, tested by Gary Becker.[59] But his results also imply that the smoker makes choices with due consideration to the addictive properties of tobacco. This brings addiction within the framework of rational choice: the consumer who chooses to smoke judges that the satisfaction he derives from smoking exceeds the actual and future costs of addiction, otherwise, he will smoke less or quit. From this perspective, state intervention to prevent or break addiction is only paternalism at another level.

Individual choices are not always optimal, but neither are the paternalistic state's coercive interventions. We too often fall into the trap of comparing real individuals with the state as it should be or, even more

---

59  Gary S. Becker, Michael Grossman, and Kevin M. Murphy, An Empirical Analysis of Cigarette Addiction, *American Economic Review*, Vol. 84, No. 3 (June 1994), pp. 396-419.

unrealistically, individuals viewed as idiots with a supposedly ideal and perfect state. There is nothing to suggest that the state has a superior capability to provide individuals with accurate information, or that its ability to make the right choices about the risks people take in their lives is necessarily better. Just as there are "market failures," there are also "government failures," and nothing suggests *a priori* that the former are more serious than the latter.[60]

## *Do Nonsmokers Pay Involuntary Costs?*

Prohibition being difficult to justify in our society when it merely aims at protecting individuals from themselves, the prohibitionists fall back on torts caused to third parties. This transmutation of a

---

60 Stephen C. Littlechild, Smoking and Market Failure, in Robert D. Tollison (Ed.), *Smoking and Society: Toward a More Balanced Assessment* (Lexington: Lexington Books, 1986), pp. 271-284.

victimless vice into a dangerous crime has previously been used in support of Prohibition in the U.S.: alcohol consumption was deemed immoral, but a particular emphasis was put on its dangers for innocent third parties.[61] Hear an American senator's plea in favor of Prohibition:

> *Whereas*, exact scientific research has demonstrated that alcohol is a narcotic poison, destructive and degenerating to the human organism, and that its distribution as a beverage or contained in foods, lays a staggering economic burden on the shoulders of the people, lowers to an appalling degree the average standard of character of our citizenship, thereby undermining the public morals and the foundations of free institutions, produces widespread crime, pauperism and insanity, inflicts disease and untimely death upon hundreds of thousands of citizens, and blights with degeneracy their children

---

61 Burt Neuborne, Prohibition and Third-Party Costs: A Suggested Analysis, in Robert D. Tollison (Ed.), *Clearing the Air: Perspectives on Tobacco Smoke* (Lexington: Lexington Books, 1988), pp. 94-98.

unborn, threatening the future integrity of the nation...[62]

Smoking is thus presented as an aggression against others. On the one hand, ETS will cause diseases in a certain number of nonsmokers. On the other hand, all nonsmokers will involuntarily pay part of the costs of smokers' illnesses. I will consider each of these two arguments in a few moments.

First, let us inquire about the conception of liberty that underlies anti-tobacco arguments. These are often based on the negation of liberty, as when the World Health Organization conceived of liberty as the power to modify the behavior of others and claimed, contrary to the general presumption of liberal law, that smoking should be forbidden unless specifically permitted.[63] Sometimes, however, the

---

62 Senator Morris Sheppard, quoted by James T. Bennet and Thomas J. Dilorenzo, *op. cit.*, p. 226.

63 See Douglas J. Den Uyl, Smoking, Human Rights, and Civil Liberties, *op. cit.*, pp. 215-216.

enemies of smoking take a more liberal route. ETS is viewed as an aggression which is simply prohibited under the old formula: your liberty stops where mine begins. An anti-tobacco activist makes this very point by stating that "Smokers' right to smoke stops where my lungs begin"[64] —just as we could say, Your liberty to throw a punch stops at my nose.

The problem with this last notion of liberty is that it is indeterminate so long as its domain has not been circumscribed. Suppose I say, "Your freedom of expression stops at my ear and my retina," this obviously implies that you have no right to express any opinion with which I am not in agreement. What we presumably mean instead, is that freedom of expression stops where the equal freedom of others begins. Now, defining an equal liberty requires underlying property rights, whose function

---

64 Steve Allen and Bill Adler, *The Passionate Nonsmokers Bill of Rights* (New York: William Morrow, 1989), p. 24.

is to precisely circumscribe the domain of liberty. My freedom of expression is to be exercised on my own property, with means that belong either to me or to some other owner who freely consents to my use of his property. The limits of liberty are defined in terms of property rights. I don't have a right to organize a press conference in your home, or to express my opinions on your Web site, or to force a newspaper to publish me.

Let's reformulate the problem in the economist's way. Some activities or exchanges generate what are called "externalities," i.e., they have positive or negative effects on third parties. Pollution falls into the class of negative externalities: I buy paper from you and, in manufacturing it, you eject particulates into the environment, which affects some third parties' enjoyment. Economists know that this kind of problem comes from the absence, or difficult enforcement, of private property rights. When well-defined property rights exist and can be enforced at not too high a cost, externalities are "internalized."[65] You are not allowed to pollute my backyard with your domestic garbage; but if you buy or otherwise obtain my consent, your garbage thrown in my backyard is not an externality anymore. By allowing free exchanges to internalize externalities, private property rights reconcile everybody's freedoms.

This is directly relevant to ETS, which, for our purposes here, we will continue to assume to have all the medical consequences claimed by government. ETS imposes a negative externality, or external cost, to nonsmokers—or, at any rate, to anti-smokers. Conversely, a non-smoking rule imposes a cost to smokers. The problem is therefore to reconcile the preferences of smokers and nonsmokers.

---

65  This is the core of the famous Coase Theorem; see Ronald Coase, The Problem of Social Cost, *Journal of Law and Economics*, Vol. 3 (October 1960), pp. 1-41.

American economist Walter Williams tells the story of a woman who asked him to put out the cigarette he had lit while waiting in a line. Williams replied, "Do you own the air?"[66] In other words, Why don't I have the right to demand that you do not forbid smoking? If property rights on the surrounding air are well-defined, it is clear who has the right to impose regulations, just as it is clear that those who do not agree with the owner bear the burden of persuading or bribing him.

In public places (like the airport terminal where Prof. Williams was standing), property rights are not well-defined since they belong to everybody in general and nobody in particular. Hence, the unavoidable conflict that Williams' question brings to light. On the contrary, private places are characterized by property rights that

---

66 Walter Williams, Tobacco and Property Rights, in Robert D. Tollison (Ed.), *Clearing the Air: Perspectives on Tobacco Smoke* (Lexington: Lexington Books, 1988, pp. 39-52), p. 39.

clearly establish who is authorized to set the rules. You own the space within your own home, so you are the one who decides to which use your air will be put. You may decide that tobacco smoke is forbidden, or that smoking is required, or that one will do as one pleases. If somebody wants to use your air differently, he must first obtain your consent, possibly by compensating you. The form of this compensation —whether it be the benefit of your guest's presence or hard cash—is a matter of the free agreement reached between you.

The solution is exactly the same in private places open to the public which are mistakenly called "public places." A restaurant owner has the right to allow his customers to smoke, to forbid it, or to make some other arrangement. If he bans smoking, he will lose some smoking customers; if he allows it, he will displease some nonsmokers. Assuming that he has no preferences of his own to which he is willing to sacrifice profits, he will adopt the most profitable rule: if he has more smoking than non-smoking customers, or if the former are willing to pay more than the latter for a congenial environment, he will operate a smoking restaurant; otherwise, he will not admit smokers. If none of the two groups is willing to compensate him for excluding the other, the owner will set up smoking and non-smoking sections, or install better ventilation. In fact, all such formulas exist on the market. The economist would say that private property has internalized the social costs of externalities that smokers impose on nonsmokers, and the symmetrical social costs that the latter impose on the former, with the result that social costs are reduced to zero.[67]

Laws regulating smoking in private places work the other way: they amount to partial nationalization of private property, prevent the reconciliation of individual

---

67 William F. Shughart II and Robert D. Tollison, Smokers versus Nonsmokers, in Robert D. Tollison (Ed.), *Smoking and Society: Toward a More Balanced Assessment* (Lexington: Lexington Books, 1986), p. 217-224.

freedoms, and forbid market diversity. In the U.S., some municipal governments now even forbid smoking in restaurants, and the Quebec government is apparently considering such prohibition.[68]

Private property rights similarly regulate other private and contractual relations, like hiring and working conditions. For example, assume—even if it is far from certain—that smokers make less productive workers than nonsmokers. In the absence of restrictive labor regulation or collective agreements, employers will make up for smokers' lower productivity by paying them lower wages. Employees who find that the pleasure of smoking is not worth the lost salary will only have to quit smoking. Contractual relations will solve in a similar way any externality that smoking employees may impose on their non-smoking colleagues. If nonsmokers are more adversely affected by a permissive

---

68 Ministère de la Santé et des Services sociaux, *op. cit.*, pp. 33-34.

rule than smokers are by prohibition—because either the former are more numerous or they have more intense preferences in this matter—it will be in their employer's interest to impose a non-smoking policy in order to maximize productivity; *mutatis mutandis* if the converse conditions apply. Of course, compromises are possible between the two extremes of total prohibition and complete permissiveness. Since the plant belongs to the employer, and workers own their labor services, property rights are well defined, and contractually agreed-on rules will take everybody's preferences into account.

It should be noted that this argument is not affected by the hypothesis that ETS is dangerous to one's health. Particular risks attached to private places are a normal feature of social relations. If you go to a ski resort that allows downhill racing (as is often the case in the Alps), you run an increased risk of being hit and injured by fast skiers. Barring any regulatory prohibition, resort owners will choose between allowing downhill skiing or not based upon their expected profits, which means that the relative intensity of skiers' preferences will dictate the trade-off. Similarly, the decision to engage in unprotected sex belongs to the individuals involved, depending on their evaluation of the pleasure gained compared to the risk of sexually transmitted diseases (including AIDS). The case of ETS is even simpler since it is usually easy to find out if others smoke. The choice of patronizing a shop, or working in a business, where smoking is allowed, belongs to each individual according to his estimated benefits versus any future costs he may risk.

Those who believe that one purpose of state intervention is to support minority preferences would think that the law should protect smokers, who now make up only a third of the Canadian population. They would reason as follows: If we allow the free interplay of markets and private property rights, smokers will be at a disadvantage. For instance, most restaurant owners will try to attract a clientele of nonsmokers—assuming that nonsmokers are not simply indifferent to tobacco smoke. The smoking minority will then have to pay more to persuade restaurants to cater to its preferences, in the same way that minority preferences often cost more to satisfy (think about left-handers). This natural discrimination will be aggravated by the fact that smokers (especially smoking men) come from the less educated and poorer classes of society.[69] In other words, smokers have less money than nonsmokers to express their preferences in the market.

Against this line of reasoning, I would argue for *laissez-faire*: the state should take no notice of private discrimination; it should neither protect smokers against

---

69 Lirio S. Covey, Edith A. Zang, and Ernst L. Wynder, Cigarette Smoking and Occupational Status, *American Journal of Public Health*, Vol. 82, No. 9, p. 1230-1234.

private discrimination nor, as it does now, enforce public discrimination against them. It is possible that the decreasing proportion of smokers and their concentration in lower social strata would lead to more smoking bans in private places. Yet, in the absence of regulatory prohibitions, it is quite possible that smokers would still be able to find hospitable places, if they attach more value to their pleasure than what nonsmokers would pay to have them excluded. It is quite possible that smokers, even with their lower incomes, are willing to pay more than nonsmokers to persuade private businesses to welcome them. Consider the case, reported in the *Wall Street Journal*, of a well-known Chicago restaurant forced to close down after the owner had banned perfume and smoking because of his allergies.[70] Of course, there is no way *a priori* to gauge the intensity of smokers' and nonsmokers' preferences, or to fore-

---

70 *Wall Street Journal*, April 6, 1995, p. A1.

cast which contractual trade-offs will ensue: letting the market work is the only way to know.

The hypothesis that smokers would compete successfully against anti-smokers for hospitable places to indulge their tastes also provides an explanation of why the latter lobby for discriminatory laws. By thus restraining competition, anti-smokers partly transfer the cost of satisfying their own preferences to smokers. From this perspective, anti-smoking laws simply amount to a political redistribution of wealth from smokers to nonsmokers, from the poor to the rich.[71]

The problem of reconciling individual preferences calls for different answers in real public places, i.e., on state properties or on the commons—spaces that belong to

---

71 See William F. Shughart II and Robert D. Tollison, Smokers versus Nonsmokers, *op. cit.*, p. 217-224; and Peter L. Berger, A Sociological View of the Antismoking Phenomenon, in Robert D. Tollison, *Smoking and Society: Toward a More Balanced Assessment* (Lexington: Lexington Books, 1986), p. 225-240.

nobody in particular and to everybody in general. In this case, private property and market mechanisms cannot work, and establishing rules of social interaction falls back either on spontaneous evolution of morals and etiquette, or on political and bureaucratic processes. Of course, ETS can present problems only in closed public places; in the streets or in public parks or forests, ETS is too diluted to carry any health risk.

In closed public places, then, the problem of tobacco usage is more complex. On the one hand, it can be argued that public places belong as much to smokers as to nonsmokers, and that there is no special reason to favor one group over the other. On the other hand, one could claim that a ban on smoking will only inconvenience smokers, while (given our starting assumption) ETS in a public place is a real aggression against nonsmokers; that excluding smokers is less consequential than subjecting nonsmokers to tobacco smoke. This is, in my opinion, the only serious argument for prohibiting smoking—but remember that it applies only in real, closed public places.

Yet, the view of ETS in public places as physical aggression which may legitimately be prohibited raises many problems. First, the connection between a mere risk and an aggression is not transparent. Every user of a public road increases your own risk of being the victim of a car accident, but this obviously does not provide a justification for keeping everybody but you off the road—especially since the argument can also be used against you by anybody else. Any person with a contagious disease poses a risk to others, but we think, and rightly so, that this does not justify the forcible quarantine of the contagious. Certain persons are more likely to commit violent crimes than others, but they are still allowed to circulate on the public domain. How, then, can smoking prohibitions be justified?

Second, if any projection of objects or particulates (like ETS particulates) on somebody else is deemed an aggression, we run into vexing problems, for this sort of interference is inseparable from social interaction. Perfumes and colognes throw off particulates within other people's noses. Should scented women therefore be barred from public places? This example is not as unrealistic as it sounds. A U.S. group of environmental health experts proclaims that "perfume pollutes." A *Wall Street Journal* reporter explains: "What cigarette smoke was to the past decade, other smells —fragrant and foul—may be to the nineties."[72] Some persons claim to be allergic to perfumes, and one can safely bet that their number would go through the roof if there were a law.

---

72 *Wall Street Journal*, May 13, 1993, p. A1.

Third, the distinction between public and private domains must again be stressed. As much as private property, by its very nature, allows owners to enforce whichever rule they may choose, however arbitrary, so should interference with individual preferences and diversity be minimized in public places. It may be argued that the minimization of arbitrary or discriminatory regulation lies at the heart of any justification for the existence of a public domain. While a private owner may choose to discriminate against smokers or nonsmokers, against perfumed or non-perfumed women, one would expect the law not to favor any specific group on the public domain. And let us add that there are means—ventilation, among others—to minimize the ETS risks.

Another argument is that conflictual and controversial actions call for legal rules. Conflictual and controversial presumably refer to an action that goes against the preferences of a large number of individuals.

In certain parts of the world, for instance, breast-feeding in public is a cause of scandal, as it subjects many people to the sight of women's breast (I assume that nobody feels assaulted by the sight of a baby's mouth). Now, to the very extent that many individuals share such attitudes, rules of etiquette and expressions of social disapprobation will develop to solve the conflict between breast-feeding women and offended eyes. Such spontaneous rules and practices make political edicts superfluous. Indeed, appeals to the force of law suggest that the relevant majority (or minority) is not numerous enough to generate informal rules, but it is politically powerful enough to redistribute power in its favor.

This being said, ETS does raise a problem in real public places—assuming again that it is dangerous to nonsmokers' health.[73] The conflictual nature of public property justifies privatizing public places

---

73 See Douglas J. Den Uyl, Smoking, Human Rights, and Civil Liberties, *op. cit.*, pp. 203-204.

whenever they are not essential for on-going, free social cooperation. A large part of the problem we are dealing with here comes more from the nature of the public domain than from the risks of ETS. Solutions should address the root problem, which is the ubiquitous presence of the State, and its nationalization of a large portion of space. As far as essential public places are concerned, we can only hope for imperfect regulations that should aim at reconciling all users' preferences, and balancing normal requirements of social life with risks of torts. This is why, in real, closed public places, the actual magnitude of ETS risks is relevant: the lower the risk, the less justified an intervention.

I have argued that ETS imposes no externality on nonsmokers on private property, and that whatever externality it generates in public places is inseparable from social life—except if it implies important torts, and if the existence of such public places is justified. The second part of the externality argument deals with the possibility that nonsmokers support part of the tobacco-related health costs of smokers. The argument comes in two versions: one is naive, the other faulty.

The naive version considers all the costs of smokers' tobacco-related diseases—mainly medical costs and productivity loss—as a social loss. This is naive because the costs that the smokers themselves support are not social, but individual, costs. It's the smoker himself who pays for what "society" loses. If a smoker's illness and premature death cut his income by, say, $200,000, this corresponds exactly to lost production in society. At the margin, an individual's income equals the value of his production, so that the loss of this production by "society" is totally supported by the non-producing culprit (and possibly by those other individuals who had voluntarily chosen to depend on his income). Society is not penalized and it's none of its business—unless we think that it owns individuals. Similarly, if a sick smoker himself pays for his medical care, or if he has purchased private insurance (which may cost more because of his vices), he thus supports all the so-called "social costs" of his illness.

A less naive version of the social cost argument invokes the fact that certain costs of tobacco-related diseases, especially medical costs, have been socialized through public health and assistance programs. Hence, all taxpayers, including nonsmokers, are penalized by the smokers' risks. This argument can be criticized from both an empirical and a theoretical standpoint.

It is empirically doubtful that smokers' diseases transfer costs to nonsmokers, for it can be shown that the net public costs of all smokers' diseases that fall on non-smoking taxpayers ($207 million in Canada, in 1986) are more than offset by two compensating factors: tobacco taxes that have been redistributed to nonsmokers ($3.2 billion); and public pension savings ($1.4 billion) from smokers' reduced life expectancy. These estimates, by Raynauld and Vidal,[74] mean not only that there is no net cost imposed by smokers on nonsmoking taxpayers, but that the transfer actually goes the other way: nonsmoking taxpayers benefit from a $4.3-billion annual transfer from smokers.

Even if we rely on the federal Department of Health's own estimate for the public cost of tobacco-related diseases, i.e., three billion dollars per year (instead of $207 million), we still have a net transfer from smokers to nonsmokers. The existence of this transfer is confirmed by many U.S. studies (in the case of alcohol, interestingly, the transfer works the other way:

---

74 André Raynauld and Jean-Pierre Vidal, Smokers' Burden on Society: Myth and Reality in Canada, *Canadian Public Policy*, Vol. 13, No. 3 (1992), pp. 300-317.

from non-drinkers to drinkers).[75] The federal Department of Health draws a different conclusion because, following the naive approach, it boosts social costs by some eight billion dollars from smokers' lost productivity and income.[76]

From a theoretical and methodological standpoint, it is not permissible to include in social costs even that part of smokers' health costs that is paid for by non-smoking taxpayers. Nonsmokers support these costs only because the state has (more or less) nationalized the health care industry—with the likely support of a majority of nonsmokers. The abolition of private property and freedom of contract in this industry generates artificial externalities: when society claims the ownership of everyone's health, everyone supports

---

75 See especially William Manning *et al.*, The Taxes of Sin: Do Smokers and Drinkers Pay Their Way? *Journal of the American Medical Association*, Vol. 211 (March 17, 1989), pp. 1604-1609; James T. Bennet and Thomas J. Dilorenzo, *op. cit.*, p. 228.

76 Health Canada, *op. cit.*, pp. 17-18.

everyone else's costs. One's life-style may then be viewed as an externality for others. A serious study published in the *American Journal of Public Health* provides a case in point, as it purports to show that the health care costs of those who do not exercise enough impose externalities to less sedentary taxpayers.[77] Such a perverted logic justifies controlling or taxing not only tobacco and alcohol, but also sedentary life-styles, driving, skiing, diet, sexual relations, and so forth.

Actual public policies in the matter of tobacco mean nothing but legalized discrimination against smokers. This discrimination is observable not only in tax transfers from smokers to nonsmokers, but also, more directly, in the legalized segregation of smokers on both public and private properties. Let's pause on this great absurdity of our times: the same

---

77 Emmett B. Keeler *et al.*, The External Costs of a Sedentary Life-style, *American Journal of Public Health*, Vol. 79, No. 8 (August 1989), pp. 975-981.

governments that prohibit all private discrimination, institute legal apartheid
against smokers. When future historians
narrate the story of workers pushed out-
doors for a smoke, they will likely view
today's smokers as modern niggers.

# 3.
# The Costs of State Intervention

## *Economic Costs*

State interventions in tobacco markets are numerous, and range from taxes to the regulation of consumption, marketing and advertising. An economic estimate of the cost of these interventions would neglect simple transfers and try to measure what is called the "social loss" brought about by shifts in demand and supply curves of tobacco products. From the economist's point of view, the objective is to estimate the net value (net of production costs) to consumers, in terms of their own preferences, of tobacco products that state intervention keeps out of the market. Such an evaluation is methodologically and statistically complex and, to my knowledge, has never been attempted. But it is a fair bet to say that the estimated costs would be high.

In addition to economic costs in the strict sense used above, state intervention also produces unintended effects (*"effets pervers"* in French). Like any interference in delicate and complex social processes, tobacco regulations will often have consequences that run counter to official objectives. One of these unintended consequences lies in the appeal of the forbidden, especially among the young. While the proportion of smokers among American teenagers was dropping fast during the 70s, it is now apparently on the rise.[78] The Canadian government admits that "smoking

---

78  Surgeon General, *op. cit.*, p. 9 and Table 15 (p. 75); and *Wall Street Journal*, April 16, 1996, p. B5.

uptake is increasing among young Canadi-ans, particularly young women."[79] In Quebec, we are told that 32% of young people smoked in 1994, compared to 20% in 1991.[80]

Some critics also argue that ridiculous government propaganda on ETS is dilut-ing the perceived dangers of tobacco, and perhaps even of hard drugs, thus stimulat-ing their consumption.[81] But the ultimate illustration of the perverse consequences of state moralization is provided in a *Wall Street Journal* report on a new phenome-non: forbidden tobacco promoted to sexual fantasy. Pornographic videos have hit the market, featuring fully clothed women who sensually inhale and exhale cigarette smoke. An Internet newsgroup is

---

79 Health Canada, *op. cit.*, p. 4.
80 Ministère de la Santé et des Services sociaux, *op. cit.*, p. 8. However, these statistics include a high proportion of occa-sional smokers and, like much data in this report, are diffi-cult to interpret.
81 Christopher Caldwell, Smoke Gets in Your Eyes, *op. cit.*, p. 28.

called "atl.sex.fetish.smoking." According to the editor of a fetishist magazine, "Smoking is the fetish of the '90s."[82]

## *Costs in terms of Liberty*

What I wish to emphasize here are the immaterial and hidden costs of state intervention for our already greatly threatened liberties. Prohibition of, or prohibitionist regulations against, any peaceful activity always means dangerous and unwarranted growth in state power. Tobacco illustrates this phenomenon which, I fear, has yet to reach its zenith. I will mention only some of the most obvious instances. Public control of private consumption and production of tobacco strikes another blow at private property rights. Regulation of tobacco advertising provides the state with new opportunities for censorship and propaganda. The development of black

---

82 *Wall Street Journal*, January 31, 1996, pp. A1 and A4.

markets in tobacco products offers good excuses for more police powers and a strengthening of the heavy hand of the state. As the Quebec Department of Health's discussion paper puts it, the fight against tobacco "calls for a plan of economic, social and cultural 'reengineering'."[83]

When people go along with all this in order to protect individuals from themselves, or when they accept the manipulation of science in the name of imaginary victims, then nobody should be surprised that the state feels justified to prohibit anything. The founder of an anti-caffeine movement in the country of the EPA speaks to this point: "In five years, coffee is going to be treated just like nicotine."[84] Today, prohibition of smoking in any place legally defined as "public"; tomorrow,

---

83 Ministère de la Santé et des Services sociaux, *op. cit.*, p. 22: "À cet égard, c'est une 'réingénierie' économique, sociale et culturelle qu'il faut planifier."

84 *Wall Street Journal*, January 13, 1995, p. A1 and A6.

why not, prohibition in private homes or vehicles?[85]

Another dimension of the hidden costs of state intervention in tobacco relates to the new puritanism spreading over the world. Closing one's eyes to the benefits that come with the costs of smoking is not always the mere consequence of the kind of analytical error pointed out above: in some people's minds, pleasure is a sin, nothing but a cost.

There is nothing new under the sun. Like alcohol, tobacco was first scourged on moral grounds. Popes Urban II and Innocent XII forbade tobacco in churches under penalty of excommunication. King James I also stands among the first modern prohibitionists. Cardinal Richelieu and Queen Victoria opposed smoking.[86] During the 1890s, many American State

85 See *Wall Street Journal*, September 22, 1994, p. A24.

86 See Bertrand Deveaud and Bertrand Lemennicier, *op. cit.*, p. 38; Walter Williams, Tobacco and Property Rights, *op. cit.*, p. 39.

governments prohibited tobacco, and some still forbid smoking by minors.[87] Even if such existing laws are not enforced any more, they show the connection between puritanism and the infamy cast on tobacco. Alexis de Tocqueville took note of how puritanism in early American colonies had produced legal prohibitions of blasphemy, adultery, and tobacco. In *Democracy in America*, he says of the legislator: "Sometimes indeed the zeal of his enactments induces him to descend to the most frivolous particulars: thus a law is to be found in the same Code [Connecticut's Code of 1650] which prohibits the use of tobacco." From his democratic perspective, he adds:

> It must not be forgotten that these fantastical and vexatious laws were not imposed by authority, but that they were freely voted by all the persons interested, and

---

87 See Richard Klein, *Cigarettes are Sublime* (Durham and London: Duke University Press, 1993), p. 4; Surgeon General, *op. cit.*, p. 247; and Frank Rose, If It Feels Good, It Must Be Bad, *Fortune*, October 21, 1991, p. 91 ff.

that the manners of the community were even more austere and more puritanical than the laws. In 1649 a solemn association was formed in Boston to check the worldly luxury of long hair.[88]

Some anti-tobacco movements remain essentially religious, such as that among Muslim fundamentalists, for instance.[89] In our own countries, the content of morals has changed from religious to social and scientific or, more exactly, to socialist and pseudo-scientific. From a comparative

---

88 Alexis de Tocqueville, *Democracy in America* (1835), Volume 1 (New York: Colonial Press, 1899), p. 38; *De la Démocratie en Amérique*, Vol. 1 (1835), Part I, Chap. 2 (Paris: Laffont, 1986, p. 69): "Quelquefois, enfin, l'ardeur réglementaire qui [...] possède [le législateur] le porte à s'occuper des soins les plus indignes de lui. C'est ainsi qu'on trouve dans le même code [le Code du Connecticut de 1650] une loi qui prohibe l'usage du tabac. [...] Il ne faut pas, au reste, perdre de vue que ces lois bizarres ou tyranniques n'étaient point imposées; qu'elles étaient votées par le libre concours de tous les intéressés eux-mêmes, et que les moeurs étaient encore plus austères et plus puritaines que les lois. À la date de 1649, on voit se former à Boston une association solennelle ayant pour but de prévenir le luxe mondain des longs cheveux."

89 William F. Shughart II and Robert D. Tollison, Smokers versus Nonsmokers, *op. cit.*, p. 239.

historical viewpoint, today's conventional wisdom about tobacco is reminiscent of the late 19th-century scientific community harboring a large consensus about the harmful character of masturbation.[90] The alliance between the new puritanism and the state is all the more dangerous given the realization of Tocqueville's predictions, i.e., the incredibly more refined administrative crisscrossing by the contemporary state—compared to the means at the disposal of former princes—and its growing threat to privacy and individual autonomy.

Although puritan or moralizing states were not always totalitarian, despotic governments naturally jump on the moralization bandwagon. "German women do not smoke" (*Deutschen Weiben rauchen nicht*), claimed a Nazi slogan.[91] Adolf Hitler, a former smoker himself, had developed a

---

90 Burt Neuborne, Prohibition and Third-Party Costs: A Suggested Analysis, op. cit., p. 94.
91 Quoted by Richard Klein, *op. cit.*, p. 12.

detailed vision of the perfect Nazi's morals, which included vegetarianism and a hatred of alcohol and tobacco. "I asked Göring," he said, "if he really thought it a good idea to be photographed with a pipe in his mouth."[92] He blamed the military high command for distributing tobacco rations, which he intended to abolish after the war: "We can make better use of our foreign currency than squandering it on imports of poison."[93] Hitler was also quite ahead of his times by forbidding smoking in his office:

> I made the acquaintance in Bayreuth of a business man ... There was a notice on his door: "Smokers not admitted." For my part, I have no notice above my door, but smokers aren't admitted.[94]

Hitler even anticipated our own anti-smoking campaigners with the following

---

92 Adolf Hitler, *Hitler's Table Talk 1941-1944* (London: Weidenfeld and Nicolson, 1953), p. 360-361.

93 *Ibid.*, p. 360-361.

94 *Loc. cit.*

actual complaint, which was probably as scientific as today's propaganda:

> When I go into an inn where people are smoking, within an hour I feel I've caught a cold. The microbes hurl themselves upon me! They find a favorable climate in the smoke and heat.[95]

Richard Klein suggests that dissenters and revolutionary movements have always, on the contrary, claimed the right to produce, sell and consume tobacco.[96] Poets even linked tobacco to metaphysical revolt, as illustrated by Jules Laforgue's beautiful verses[97]:

> Et pour tuer le temps, en attendant la mort,
> Je fume au nez des dieux de fines cigarettes.

The deresponsibilization of the individual represents another hidden cost of state intervention and wardship. Although

---

95 *Ibid.*, p. 231-232.

96 Richard Klein, *op. cit.*, p. 12.

97 Jules Laforgue, "La cigarette" (1880): quoted by Richard Klein, *op. cit.*, p. 57-58:
"And to kill time while awaiting death,
I smoke slender cigarettes thumbing my nose to the gods."

this phenomenon and its impact are difficult to measure, the substitution of state addiction for the individualist sentiment is visible everywhere. Growing addicted to the state is a recursive process which justifies more state controls and still more dependency.[98] Now, given the state's responsibility for wars and other historical catastrophes, this addiction is more dangerous than any herb one can think of.

Historically in our culture, smoking has not been a rude or disgusting habit — like, for instance, blowing one's nose at the dinner table, or spitting. As witnessed by Molière's praise of tobacco, Baudelaire's poem on "an author's pipe," or more contemporary vindications by Jean-Jacques Brochier[99] or Richard Klein, Nicot's herb

---

98 See Pierre Lemieux, *The Individualist Sentiment*, speech given at the Junto Meeting, Niederhoffer & Niederhoffer, New York City, February 1, 1996; reprinted in *Arms, Law & Society*, No. 5 (Spring 1996), p. 1-18 and, in Spanish, in *biTarte*, Vol. 4, No. 9 (August 1996), p. 9-21; also available at http://www.spinnaker.com/Pierre_Lemieux.

99 Jean-Jacques Brochier, *Je fume, et alors?* (Paris: Belles Lettres, 1990).

occupies an honorable place in the history of the civilization that discovered liberty. It is therefore not surprising that civility has long required that a guest be allowed to smoke by his host, at the mere cost of asking for permission, which could not be refused except for serious reasons, and never on the basis of a whim or in order to make a political point.

Irrational emotions against smoking and the return of puritanism under the guise of political correctness have thus, at least in America, contributed to the decline of civility. The point here is not to question the right of anybody to ban smoking, or anything else, in his own home, as this liberty provides an irreplaceable mechanism for reconciling individual preferences. But one cannot avoid the impression that, by promoting intolerance towards smokers— our modern niggers—the state has, in this field as in others, worked towards undermining the spontaneous rules of civilization, which are of the nature of public goods.

# Epilogue

After echoing a few scientific doubts about the danger of tobacco, and especially the very fleeting ETS, I have tried to show that, even if we accept the dreadful claims of government propaganda, coercive public regulation of production and consumption of tobacco has no rational basis but the glorification of state paternalism and its growing power. As we know it at the end of the 20th century, the state is, much more than tobacco, a very real public health problem.

A little imagination shows two different worlds that we can leave to our children. In one of these worlds, people fear everything and the shadow of everything, except the state which, for their own good, imprisons them in the "administrative tyranny" that Tocqueville had foreseen. This world is calm and cool, but dull, savorless, smokeless, and odorless. Product packaging has been standardized, and authority has posted warnings and "forbidden" signs everywhere. Politically correct newspeak[100] has substituted sexual harassment for flirtation, alcoholism for enjoying wine, nicotine delivery devices for cigarettes, and risk for pleasure.

The second world stands at the opposite pole, with its colorful diversity, liberty and responsibility. Every individual lives his life as he sees fit, assuming the risks of his joys and the anguish of his death. Instead of devices delivering nicotine, caffeine or ethanol to human resources glued

---

100 In George Orwell's *Nineteen Eighty-Four* (London: Secker & Warburg, 1949), "newspeak" is the state-manipulated language in which dissent is properly unrepresentable and unthinkable.

to their social functions, it features individuals who smoke, sip black coffee, and drink Bordeaux wine.

There is a common denominator between these two worlds: the mortality rate is 100% in both. But the men who live and die are not the same: in the first case, they are slaves; in the second, free individuals.

Montreal, Spring 1996

# About the Author

Pierre Lemieux was born in Sherbrooke (Quebec, Canada) in 1947, and has become well-known for defending individual liberty over the last quarter of a century. His books, published by major Parisian publishers such as the Presses Universitaires de France, have been translated into many languages. He

has been cited in numerous works of political theory and in encyclopaedias as a reference point for the new liberal thought. Pierre Lemieux is also a frequent contributor to both the French and American press.

When he began his writing career, the issues he discussed, which can no longer be avoided, were basically unheard of in Quebec. He talked about libertarians at a time when almost everyone thought that the state was man's best friend.

Pierre Lemieux has his own Web site at http://www.spinnaker.com/Pierre_Lemieux.

Printed in January 1998 by

in Boucherville, Quebec